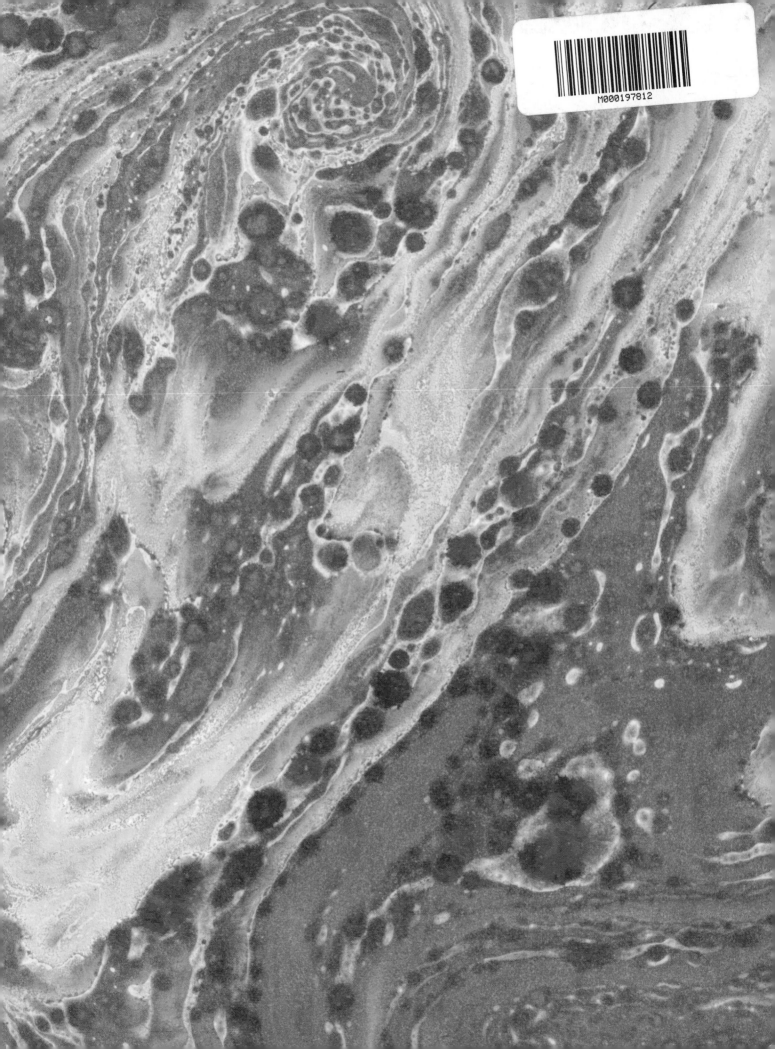

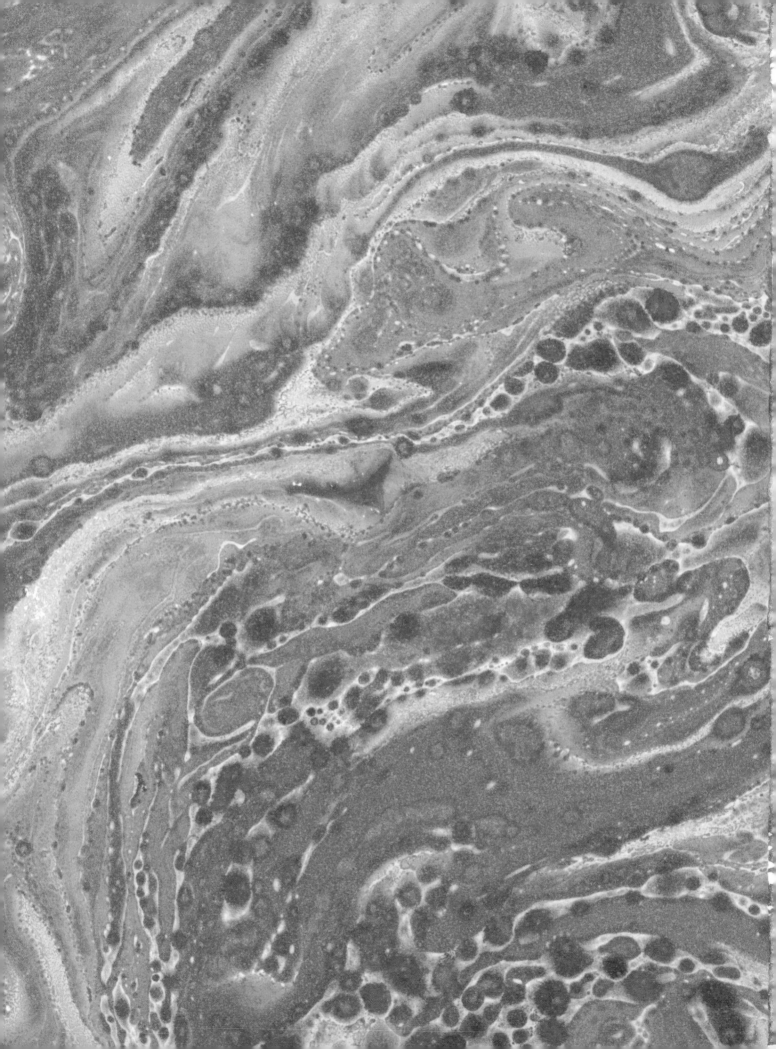

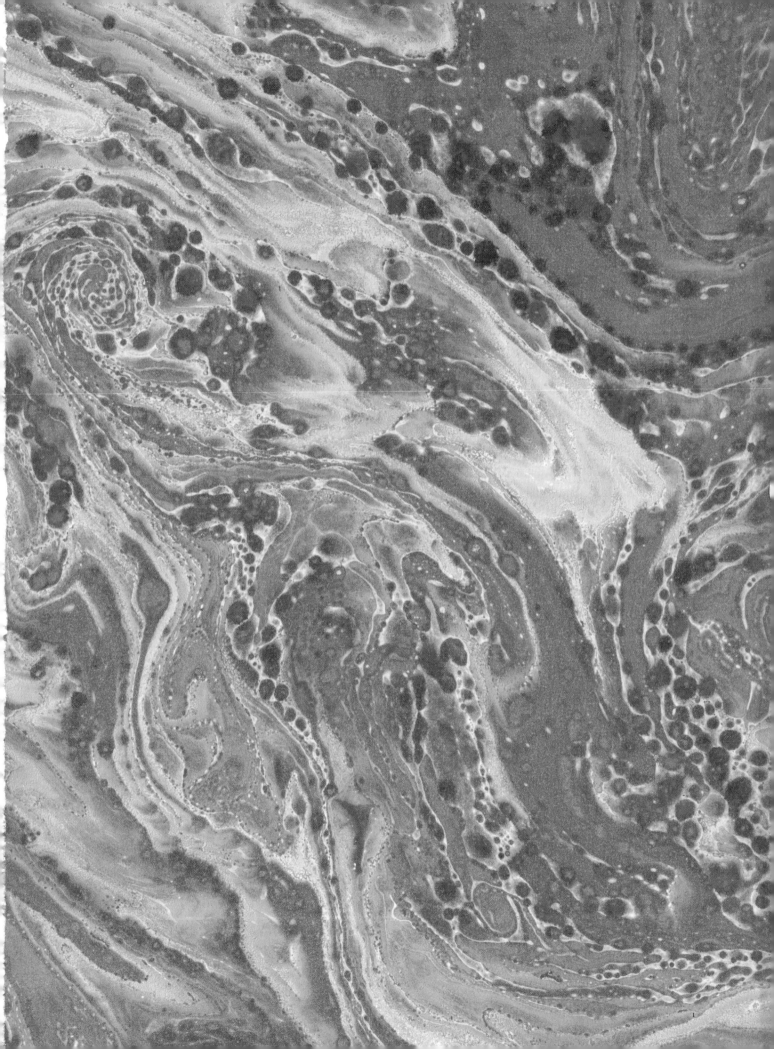

# OLD HOME
# LOVE

# OLD HOME LOVE

ANDY AND CANDIS MEREDITH

GIBBS SMITH
TO ENRICH AND INSPIRE HUMANKIND

FOR OUR LITTLE ONES
*Parker, James, Cohen, Will,*
*Tommy, Brooks and Kit.*

YOU ARE THE REASON WE MAKE THINGS BEAUTIFUL, YOU ARE OUR WHOLE HEARTS.

Published by
Gibbs Smith
P.O. Box 667
Layton, Utah 84041

1.800.835.4993 orders
www.gibbs-smith.com

Library of Congress Control Number:
2016952360

ISBN: 978-1-4236-4652-5

21 20 19 18 17     5 4 3 2 1

# CONTENTS

12

132

60

168

104

236

# WE REALLY LOVE OLD HOMES

*I never gave much thought to historic homes and their significance. I was used to seeing the pioneer homes in Utah, but to me it seemed like most of them were either in downtown areas of the smaller cities and being used as run-down rentals or in the super-exclusive avenues section of Salt Lake City.*

There wasn't a lot of in-between for these homes, and since I didn't really know anyone in either of those places, I just didn't spend time around them. I grew up hearing the stories of the people of this time and their lives and accomplishments but didn't really stop to think about their immediate surroundings, their day-to-day routines, or their homes. I have always been fascinated by the 1800s. It was such an incredible century of transformation for America and

the world. I'm sure that everyone through history tends to romanticize the past and I guess I'm no different. I'm not saying I'd like to have lived then, by any means; I really do enjoy my Bluetooth headphones.

Candis is asked all the time why she loves old homes so much and why she does what she does. Her response is simple: she was born to do it. She bought her first historic home at twenty-one and never looked back. She attributes a lot of her courage to her Grandpa Leo and Grandma Mary. Leo has fiercely loved her since she was born and built her her first playhouse; Mary is an artist who specializes in paintings of historic homes and a very strong woman herself. They taught Candis to be tough, independent, and hardworking. She was drawing floor plans for dream homes with secret floors and nooks when she was five and she would save all the old homes if she could. I think she would like to live in the 1800s if it were possible, even though she would promptly want to come back to a place where women have rights and a voice, ha-ha!

Before I met Candis, I was a full-blown adult, having lost most of that desire for exploration and discovery that we naturally have as kids. Being able to find that again in these homes has been amazing and redemptive. She really did save me. I had been through some really hard times and she showed me the brightness and beauty of life and I will always be grateful to her for that. Plus she's really cute. We brought together our little family and have been happy. Having six boys between us was an adventure, but we decided to be straight crazy and add a little girl. No regrets.

For us, these house projects have been a natural part of our relationship from the beginning. We planned our wedding at the first home we restored together while we were there working through the night, scraping wallpaper and trenching walls for electrical. We were married on the front porch and loved taking our somewhat curious/somewhat terrified wedding guests on a progress tour of the house. We have loved raising our kids in homes that people built with their own hands over several years' time, homes where we have found treasures from the past that tell the stories of a different time in the very same place.

On many a day when the unavoidable expression "Dad, I'm bored" was uttered, I handed the poor entertainment-deprived child a shovel and we went outside to the backyard to dig up the hundred-year-old trash piles scattered under the grass and dirt. I love to see their faces light up when they catch a glimpse of something in the dirt and pull out a marble or doll part that hasn't seen sunlight since Honest Abe was president. Of course, with six boys younger than thirteen, we have the constant comparison of who got the better digging implements and complaints of claim jumping and who saw the big piece of china first, but that's normal, right? We have found gold, diamonds, glass, toys, buttons, tools and all kinds of things. That's just one of the gifts these houses give. It's like growing up in an *Indiana Jones* movie.

Then we have the houses themselves. Walking the floors is a humbling experience. I don't know when I became a sentimentalist as far as homes are concerned. I just blame Candis. New homes are great. I've built one. There is something, however, about being in a place with history, a place that has seen births, deaths and so much life. I sometimes stand in a quiet historic home we are renovating and just think about the things that happened in the world and how they affected the people of that place. People gathered in that very room to discuss the assassination of President Lincoln, the excitement of in-home electrical power, indoor plumbing, automobiles and innumerable inventions, wars, discoveries and events that changed the world. It is a humbling experience that we feel fortunate to have.

We are so lucky to work together, doing something that we absolutely love. Our life is stressful, full of deadlines and large sums of money that can be won or lost, but it's our passion for these homes that keeps us moving forward. Our passion for the past and the stories of the future, our children's included, encourage us every day to risk it all for these homes and what they mean to us. We hope *Old Home Love* will give you an idea of what we feel for these houses.

*Andy and Candis Meredith*

BUILT IN 1859

# LOVE HOUSE

*Built by Mayor Leonard Harrington and his son for their family, this home in a small Utah town took nearly two years to build and was completed in 1859. It is a rare 1850s "Prairie L-Shape" adobe home. In a time when most dwellings in the area were single-room log houses, this home stood out as a masterpiece.*

We bought this house as our first home together. We wanted a place for our new blended family to have a fresh start—somewhere that was new to just us. We wanted a house filled with love—thus the name Love House. We were married here, brought our baby girl home from the hospital here and have enjoyed countless memories within the thick adobe walls.

Before we bought the house, it had fallen into severe disrepair and was slated for demolition. It was considered the worst house in the neighborhood (maybe the whole town) and most people had forgotten how special it was. We spent nearly a year bringing it back to life and are honored to be a part of its history—we are so lucky we got to save it.

### LOVE HOUSE TODAY

Many people ask why we painted the house black, thinking it is a very modern thing to do. In reality, black was a common house color in the 1800s.

 OT EVERYONE UNDERSTANDS the love and devotion we show to historic homes. All too often an old home that could be repaired is torn down instead due to the perception of it being "too much work" or being a money pit. In truth, there are times when it does cost a little more or takes a little more time to save versus starting over, but there is something tangibly significant about the way it feels to bring something back to life. Not to mention, these older homes were often, quite simply, built better.

Materials today are tricky. Some have improved greatly, like insulation, efficient windows, etc., but others have really seen a decline. The best example is that of modern lumber. Historic homes were built with old-growth timber (something we just can't, and probably shouldn't, get today). New studs are made from young, overwatered trees that lack the strength that old wood has. We think it's important to save what's left rather than seeing it end up in a landfill—that's our goal and purpose; that's why we show these old homes so much love.

## NEW OLD CHARACTER

Love House was a mess when we started—literally. It was stacked to the ceiling with garbage, among other things we won't mention. It took a little bit of vision to look past the mess and see that we were lucky to still have the original doors, trim, and by some miracle, kitchen cabinets. We restored the cabinets with a lot of sanding, puttying and painting. In the living room we added this lovely fireplace surround made with modern materials to house an electric fireplace. We were careful to make sure that it went well with the home's original features and brought enough character to fit in with the old.

**LD CLAWFOOT TUBS** are a staple in almost all of our renovations. In our opinion, it is somewhat life-changing to take a long soak in an old cast-iron tub. We rarely refinish them on the inside for two reasons: we like the natural patina of time, and we don't like things to be *so clean* that you have to maintain a level of perfection. We simply paint the outside with chalkboard paint to give it a beautiful matte finish.

We exposed the original adobe wall, above, to act as a focal point in the kitchen. The large cast-iron sink protects the adobe from water and we love seeing what the house is made of.

### ADOPTED ANCESTORS

We always look for antique portraits because they are usually inexpensive. We adopt these people into our old home family.

### PAINTED FLOORS

Painting floors is a great way to bring a pop of color and whimsy to a space. We have painted floors mustard, sky blue, navy, black, mint green and pink, to name a few. We never feel guilty painting a floor; the original is still underneath, ready to be sanded and stained when the time comes.

### ORIGINAL MIXED WITH NEW

Not everything can be original, so we add new elements when we have to (e.g., a new chandelier that looks old or new rim lock hardware that mimics the original). When we do have original features, like this staircase, we keep all of the imperfections but try to do a great paint job to update it just enough.

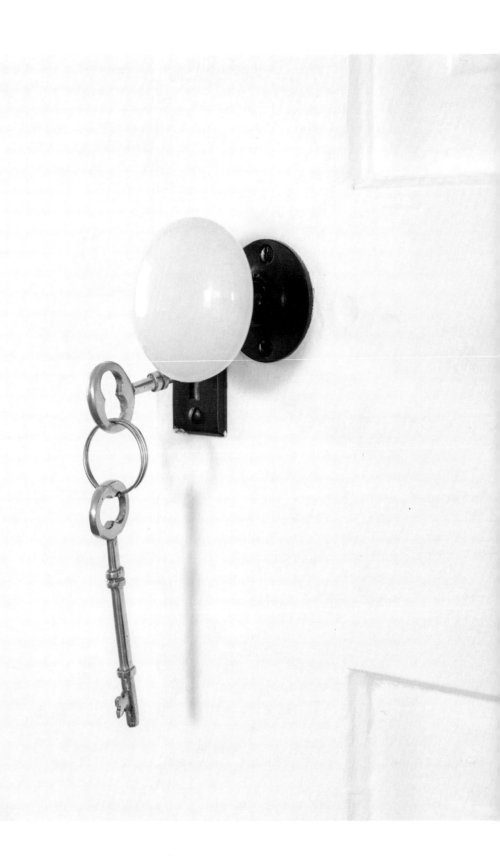

## PAINT DRAMA

The office walls painted in Farrow & Ball "Studio Green" add a bit of drama to a home that is mostly white inside. In the room behind, picture-less gold-leaf frames are stacked against the wall to create a cluster of large objects that includes the chair. A modern lamp adds height to the grouping and with a small picture above, it's a look we like; we aren't afraid to challenge scale in this way.

## PAINT COMBINATIONS

We seldom paint a house exterior or interior with more than two, sometimes three, colors. Keeping the palette simple allows the home's architecture and style to be the main focus.

## OLD PORCHES

Contractors stop by all the time and offer to fix this porch, but we left it as we found it because we like to think of all the kids who have played here over the last hundred years. When we dig around, we find marbles and bits of broken dolls; our own kids have lost Legos here. Things don't always need to look brand new.

MODERN CLASSIC STYLE

# SNOW HOUSE

*This house is a perfect example of how you can infuse your own style and aesthetic into a historic home. Sally Snow, the homeowner, lovingly restored this home; she was careful to choose timeless finishes and features, making it ready for its next hundred years.*

Built around 1930, this charming little cottage had been remodeled and stripped of its original, albeit simple, character sometime in the 1960s or '70s. Sally knew she had something special that was also perfect for her refined style.

It is not a large home nor does it have overstated architectural features, but it is absolutely stunning in its simplicity. The shake shingles and neutral color palette disguise the fact that it has been remodeled, making it seem like it has always retained its original materials and character.

### SHAKE SHINGLES

Naturally aged shake shingles add almost instant character to a new remodel. After only a year or two, these shingles will look like they have always been there.

IVY AND BOXWOODS
These plantings give the property a classic, timeless look.

*Although the home seems small,* a vaulted ceiling gives it a sense of
loftiness. The creamy white walls add even more visual space. We love
the simple and understated *design that will never go out of style;*
a custom sisal rug ties the whole room together.

SNOW HOUSE

## SIZE DOESN'T ALWAYS MATTER

Some spaces are so charming that they more than make up for their lack of square
footage. Not everyone needs a massive kitchen; in truth, we will trade a smaller
kitchen (less to clean) in order to get a larger living space.

 **HAT YOU FILL YOUR HOUSE** with is a reflection of you. This beautiful dining room has the actual buffet from the movie *The Sound of Music* along with wrought iron chairs found at a yard sale, which, incredibly, turned out to be priceless antiques! Every piece tells a story and fills a home with love.

**MASTER SUITE:** The master suite is restful and beautiful. Built-in closets on either side provide generous storage and the bathroom is conveniently nearby yet separated from the sleeping quarters by a short passageway.

## SPECIAL ANTIQUE PIECES
Although they aren't as functional as new pieces might be,
antiques add depth and patina that new just cannot match.

### THINGS THAT YOU LOVE

These antique chairs were a yard sale find for about $500 and it turns out they are extremely rare, worth $45,000 each! Classic landscaping adds character and dimension to the residence. Sally lives with her antique dishes, enjoying and using them every day.

### OVERLEAF

The wall in the office is fitted with a set of antique wood panels. Architectural salvage is a wonderful way to bring instant character to a new (or old) space.

# GARBETT HOMES

*This historic mansion is a stunning example of classic architecture and presence.*
*It sits atop Capitol Hill in Salt Lake City and maintains many of its original and*
*decorative features. The large columns and oversized dentil molding add to its*
*overall beauty and character.*

It has served many purposes: a home, an apartment, and now an office building for Garbett Homes, a new-home builder. It has been lovingly preserved and maintained by the current owner. We think it is impressive for a company to take a house like this for their office, thoughtfully and respectfully leaving the details that make up the soul of the home.

### UPDATING TO CODE

Instead of taking out the original porch rail along the balcony, which is too short to pass modern building code, they added height to make it safe. Solutions like this keep historic homes intact without sacrificing important updates.

 OMETIMES A HISTORIC HOME'S WORST ENEMY is being on too large of a lot, too close to the center of town. In the name of "progress," many homes are torn down to make way for larger commercial buildings or multi-unit housing. While we understand that people sometimes feel like this is necessary, we would never consider knocking over an old house or building.

We hope to share enough education and resources to help developers make better decisions. We are developers ourselves and try to create unique properties with old homes and buildings, much like this one, which is offices on the lower levels and a home and apartment on the upper two floors.

 SO MUCH IS WORTH
PRESERVING IN OLD HOMES—
ESPECIALLY ORIGINAL
STAINED GLASS.

EXPOSED BRICK
The old brick, original to the home,
was exposed during renovation.

**CLAIMING SPACE**
A bonus space in the turret, with original leaded glass, is used as a seating area.

MOLDINGS ADD CHARACTER AND
CHARM. DON'T BE AFRAID TO GO
"ALL OUT," EVEN IN A NEW HOME.

DENTIL, CROWN AND COLUMNS—
*layer as many as you like to achieve a unique look.*

## MATCHING ANTIQUES TO ORIGINAL DETAILS

This door frame showcases one of our favorite simple molding treatments. Antique pieces, center, finish out an authentic look for a historic home. Original features like this leaded glass, far right, are key to keeping the soul of a house intact.

A TREASURED SECOND HOME

# GOSS HOME

*In the small rural town of Spring City, Utah, are several pioneer homes restored by people who truly understand the value of a historic home saved. Seeing the hand-hauled and -placed stone, original window moldings, floors and doors is a wonderful sight.*

Spring City is a special place. The entire town has been listed on the National Register of Historic Places because of the care and attention homeowners like the Peter and Ingelise Goss family have taken to preserve its history. Without people like them, these houses may have been lost forever. The Gosses have restored this home to look as it may have in the 1800s, with every attention to detail.

The Gosses used their extensive knowledge (Peter is on the State Historic Preservation board) to re-create what had been lost and save what was left. They use this home as a peaceful getaway from their primary home in the city.

**PEACEFUL SETTING**
It's not hard to understand why the homeowners use this home as an oasis—with its serene setting and mature trees it is like a scene out of an old book.

### WOOD CEILINGS

The home has original wood-plank ceiling. In decades past, it was sometimes easier to paint a wood ceiling laid over log joists than to add a plaster ceiling.

CANDIS'S FIRST HISTORIC REMODEL

# THREE-TWENTY-THREE

*This home will always be very special to me. It was the very first historic home I renovated (save my parents' home when I was sixteen) and was also the house that my dad grew up in. My grandma sold the house when I was about twelve years old and I quietly made up my mind to buy it when I was older. I knocked on the door one day and had to beg only a little.*

We haven't been able to go through the house completely, but most of the systems have been updated, like electrical, heating and cooling, and the kitchen. Next up is the exterior.

It was so fun for me to take back the various remodels (sorry, Grandma and Grandpa) and bring it closer to its original state. Ceilings that had been dropped, shag carpeting and yellow Formica were all part of its life and are fondly remembered, but they had to go. One day I pulled off a piece of paneling and saw my grandpa's name, Emo, written in cursive paneling glue. It made me realize what an honor it had been to be a piece of this house's history.

**INEXPENSIVE UPDATES**

In the 1970s, Grandpa lovingly stripped the paint off these window trims and put up paneling. We left the paneling, added a little trim above it and painted it a lovely Dutch blue. It was a very inexpensive update and looks great!

 THE BEST PART ABOUT AN OLD HOME IS
ITS NATURAL PATINA.

# The "Give it Time" Rule

I can still remember my thoughts when I first bought this home. It was a total mixture of reverence for what Grandpa had done and a deep excitement to update, update, update!

This room belonged to my dad and his brother. Grandpa brought barn wood over from the old chicken coop and put it on the walls then decorated with red and black cowboy-themed items. It stayed that way until I was twelve years old, when the house was sold. After that it changed quite a bit, but the barn wood stayed.

When I became the new owner, I planned on taking out the barn wood because it seemed really dated; it was only my fond memories of the old cowboy room that saved it. Fast forward: reclaimed wood is now a very popular trend, and I had nearly ripped it out!

By giving something historic a little bit of time, you might be surprised at what you would have thrown away and later regretted. As a general rule, wait a year or two before deciding to remove anything historic.

A MOUNTAIN MAN HOME

# THE CABIN

*We bought Love House in a neighborhood we didn't know a lot about. As always, when we started the extensive renovation, neighbors started coming over to see what we were up to. When they realized how passionate we were about historic preservation, they said, "You've got to see the house down the street. You'll just lose your mind!"*

They were right! Just two houses down from Love House sat the most unassuming little home. The front was a modernized 1870s salt box that was charming in itself—but it was what was at the rear of the home that really took our breath away.

The back portion of the house was a completely intact mountain man trapper cabin that predates the settling of Utah by the pioneers and was being used as a master bedroom! The American Fur Company previously had a trading post right down the street. We had never seen something like this before other than at historic preservation sites. We bought the property and are getting ready to restore it this year. We plan on keeping it as a legacy to the work we are trying to do.

## ORIGINAL LOGS

This cabin is very likely the oldest in Utah and one of the few left in the state that is habitable.

# When is it too far gone?

We are probably not the best people to answer this when it comes to historic homes. In our opinion, there is almost always a way to save it. We have had devastating projects where roofs had been torn off and the house had been left to rot into the ground. Floors, moldings and windows had been removed and unwanted tenants (animals included) had moved in.

When we have moments like these, it is important that we maintain a level of perspective and respect for what we are trying to save. Most materials cannot be replicated exactly, but we can come close—we can re-create as much character as possible while still being mindful of modern conveniences. Long story short: if you have the right mind-set, it's almost never too far gone.

 Things can get worse *before they get better*. Instead of looking at the cracked plaster and dirty walls, we see *what's underneath* and what it can become.

### UPGRADING AND SAVING

There was fire damage in the bathroom. We always replace electrical in old homes; nothing can burn down a house faster than bad electrical. During construction, we go to great lengths to save and protect anything that was original to the house, such as this built-in cabinet with original glass.

Since the cabin was so close to Love House, the boys would often wander down there to swing on the rope swing and explore a *world that seemed back in time.* One day I noticed that our son James had carved his name on the cabin wall. At first I was a little upset, but then my eyes filled with happy tears knowing that *we were adding our own history* to this special place. One day soon it will be a single-family home.

# JOE JACKSON HOUSE

*When a historic home gets to remain true to its original design, the most wonderful thing happens—it takes on a character of timelessness despite very much being part of a specific time. This midcentury home is almost completely original, right down to the light switches. It's a wonderful example of the modern period in design and style.*

We don't get to restore a lot of midcentury homes because in our area they are a bit of a rarity. When we do, we welcome the challenge that this time period brings as well as the satisfaction of maintaining the beauty that the architect intended.

Joe Jackson bought this house with a bit of good luck and perseverance. Not many people can find homes like this that remain vastly untouched. It sits on top of a beautiful hill overlooking a lake and Joe is the perfect steward for such a great home. He appreciates its quirks and charms, loves its simple lines and large windows and even restores authentic period pieces to furnish it.

**THE GOOD KIND OF PANELING**
Not all wood paneling is great, especially when used in the wrong setting or time. This, however, is original to the house and so perfectly matched that it shows the grain and detail of the wood with great brilliance.

EVERY ERA OF ARCHITECTURE
HAS A STORY TO TELL.

WE COULDN'T PICK A FAVORITE
TIME PERIOD IF YOU FORCED
US. IT WOULD BE LIKE ASKING
US TO PICK A FAVORITE CHILD.

**TERRAZZO DREAM**
Terrazzo for floors and fireplace surrounds
was very popular in the midcentury when this
home was built.

**OVERLEAF**
Midcentury homes blurred the lines between
man and nature, indoors and outdoors.

## MIDCENTURY FEATURES
Capiz shell chandeliers are in style again today; this was original to this midcentury home. Built-in planters, center, were often seen in midcentury homes but are rare in modern construction, which tends to forget details like this. Terrazzo, far right, is such a beautiful original detail.

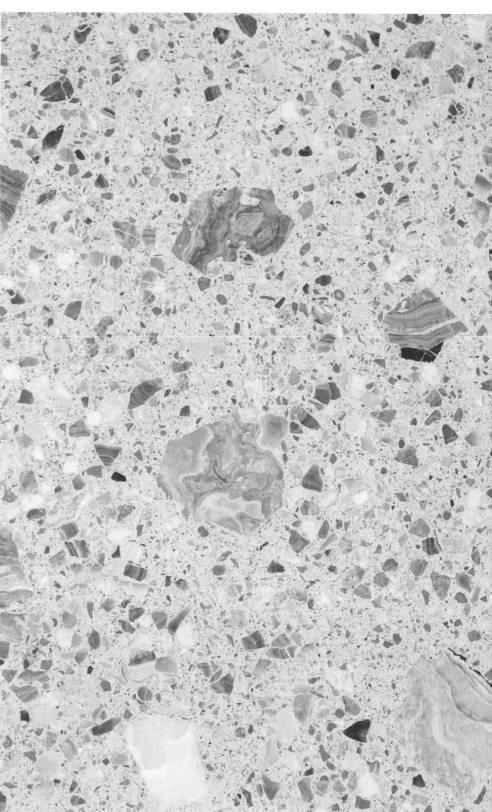

## Original Detail

Because it is so rare to have a home from any era that is virtually untouched, it is important to try to keep as many original details as you can. Joe (and the previous owners) have been so true to this home that it looks as beautiful today as it did the day it was built—maybe even better. Whenever you are considering changing something that was original to a home, ask yourself two questions: Is there a far superior material that could make my way of living significantly better? Will I regret this change, even a little, in twenty years?

## Layering Personality

Even when staying true to a home's original design, it is still important that you don't feel like you are living in a museum, paying homage to a particular time period. There were so many kinds of people alive during any given time in history. Try to identify with a type of person or style and use what works for you! We never hesitate to add our own personality in homes— we just try to make sure that it fits with the *home's* personality. It helps to choose an old home from a time period that already speaks to you.

**BUILT-IN BEAUTY**
This built-in closet is a quality feature that shows how building practices have changed over the decades. Think of the time it must have taken to build in something like this.

# MORGAN HOME

*What makes this 1920s traditional home so special is that it looks perfectly on trend while still appearing timeless. That is obviously a theme of why we love old homes so much: they are able to make a person feel like they are living in both the past and present, enjoying the best of both worlds.*

One of our favorite things about this home is the bright, colorful trim on the moldings and cabinets set against creamy white walls. They are not painted all throughout the home, just in the right places to really make the home feel unique. The cabinets are new but have a historical look in their simplicity. The lighting, furnishings, art and decor make this home feel both cozy and grand.

**PAINT FINISHES**

These cabinets look amazing not only because they are well built but also because of the perfect paint finish. When possible, we spray cabinets with a high-quality semi-gloss or gloss paint to accentuate their beauty and make the home feel fresh.

 CLASSIC FURNITURE AND ANTIQUE RUGS
HELP DRAW ATTENTION TO THE ORIGINAL
DETAILS OF A HISTORIC HOME.

## EMULATING HISTORIC CABINETS

All new floor-to-ceiling cabinets with molding at the top have been designed
to look old. The lack of counter space under the glass-front cabinets is also
a style from decades past and the blue paint makes the unit look like it has
always been there.

# Classic Decor

Some things truly never go out of style. Something we say all the time is *"If it looked good a hundred years ago, then it will look good a hundred years from now."* Toile wallpaper with painted trim is a classic look that never goes out of style.

When you are planning a renovation, keep in mind that trends come and go, but some date a home more than others. Before you put the latest modern glass tile in your kitchen, consider how it will look ten years from now, fifty years from now. If you can say you think it will look great, then do it! If not, consider using something a little more timeless—timeless, not boring! There are so many beautiful styles and materials that can still feel unique and fun.

### TIMELESS DETAILS

We've almost never seen a tufted couch that we haven't loved; this is such a timeless upholstery style. Details like this diamond cutout in the cabinet, center, add striking character to a kitchen. This simple surround with amazing tile, far right, is a treasured original part of the home.

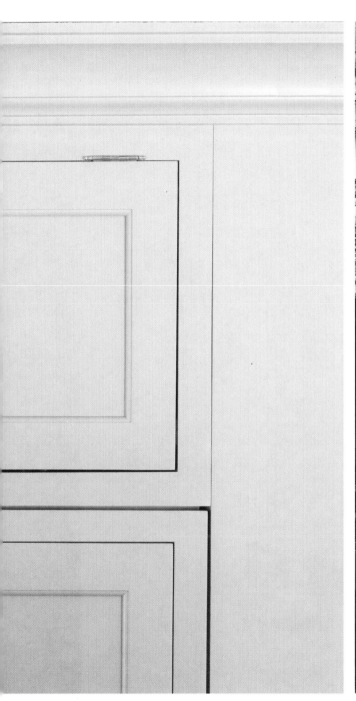

 Try to picture this foyer without all of its little details: the hardware, the inlaid floor, the moldings, the light. *Homeowners today are sometimes a bit too content* with new construction that has little or no character.

MORGAN HOME

### WHEN TO UPDATE

The bathroom, with original tile walls and built-in cabinet, got a little updating with a new sink and toilet.

In another room, white paint has given the space a bright, fresh look. Radiators painted blue look like molding.

A WORK IN PROGRESS

# OLLIE BERG HOUSE

*Our good friends had just bought their first historic home and invited us over to*
*see it. We were overjoyed for them and couldn't wait to see what they were going*
*to do with it. As we were leaving we noticed the house next door, what we now*
*call the Ollie Berg House, and knew we had to have it—had to love it back to life.*

This happens a lot with us. You never really know when you are going to find another house
to restore. We found out who the owners were and asked if they would be willing to
sell. We were in luck; they were just about to put in on the market and we were under
contract within 24 hours!

We have not started the full-scale remodel and restoration yet, but we did put a fresh coat
of white paint on the facade as a signal to passersby that this home was going to be
cared for. We did, however, finish the small apartment on the back of the home and
made it a delightful little haven.

**JUST THE FRONT**
When an old house is waiting for
us to finish other projects, we still
like to give it a little face-lift in the
meantime. On Ollie Berg, we simply
painted the facade so that neighbors
wouldn't worry about its fate.

PEELING BACK "UPDATES"

We are sometimes lucky enough to buy a home that has been untouched for a century. More often than not, though, we are left with years and years of so-called improvements that have to be removed before restoration can begin.

This adorable little kitchen is in the back of the Ollie Berg House (named after the original architect). We did a *small-budget remodel* with Ikea cabinets and subway tile—it's not always necessary to spend a lot to *make something beautiful.* The biggest impact here comes from the $100 custom shelves and $25 desk lamps-turned-sconces!

MOVED STONE BY STONE

# THE CHESTER
# SCHOOL HOUSE

*Another Spring City gem, this schoolhouse took the efforts of many local pres-*
*ervationists to get to its current site. Our good friend Zina remembers spending*
*summers as a youth moving stone after stone from the neighboring town of*
*Chester to the place the school sits today.*

Once it had been reassembled, the schoolhouse was then converted to a unique and
beautiful home. Years later, Otto Mileti became its new owner and steward. It is complete
with an open and spacious main floor and an attic suite.

Imagining a new use for an existing building takes a lot of creative thinking and planning; it
doesn't hurt to have a good amount of self-confidence to actually make the changes.

**STONE WALLS**
While moving the schoolhouse,
each and every stone was labeled,
transported and then placed back in
its exact place—a true labor of love.

**HISTORY TRANSPORTED**

It would have been so much easier to leave the school to deteriorate, but the
love and time the people gave to move it is now a remarkable part of its history.

It's fun thinking about all of the students who passed through here
when this was a school a hundred years ago; their stories live on in some
way through the historic building. Now Otto has filled his home with
*unique pieces of art and music* from his life. There is an abundance of his
personality here.

A VICTORIAN FILLED WITH ART AND LOVE

# ANDERSON HOUSE

*One of the most stunning features of this turn-of-the-century home is its commanding staircase. Its hand-carved details and original finish are absolutely breathtaking and Chris and Alison Anderson, the homeowners, have added stunning artwork to accentuate the space.*

Sometimes—meaning very rarely—we watch historic salvage television shows. They talk about how the house "has to come down" and how they are going to save as much of it as they can. I think we usually can handle about three of four minutes of it before we have to turn it off, sit quietly, and calm down.

It's so hard for us to understand why historic homes are demolished. It seems like the staircase is usually something that they "save," but it is unsettling to see something beautiful stripped from its original place of honor. We feel elated when we see a staircase like this in its original place—obviously admired and well cared for.

**LOCAL ART**
The Andersons love to collect and display art in their home. The staircase features many local artists and landscapes.

*Hand-carved newel posts* are somewhat common in old houses, but they give a staircase a distinguished look. Ornate decorative period items can be found if you are willing put in some time searching. To have something like this made today, look for a woodworking artisan and be prepared to spend some money. An original bay window, facing, is a treasure.

# What Speaks to You

We wonder if one of the reasons people prefer new homes
is because they want to make something new that is just for
them. Perhaps they feel that to personalize their space they
need to start with a clean slate.

What we love about old homes is that you really can decorate and
personalize these spaces with just a few changes or updates. The
Andersons have painted their walls a lovely cream color, but we
could also see it decorated with stark white walls and art that is more
modern. That is not their taste, but it might be yours. Old homes come
with built-in character, but that's not to say that you can't add to it!

Be adventurous and consider what you could do with an old home. Let
your story add to the home's story. Find what speaks to you and don't
be afraid the house won't accept it and love it.

**AN INVITING ENTRY**
The first thing you are greeted with when you enter this lovely home is
the staircase, art and this amazing statue. A small peek into the dining
nook shows an original and charming fireplace.

A CHARMING STONE COTTAGE

# THATCHER HOME

*We get to meet so many wonderful people through our work of renovating old houses. It is true that it takes a certain kind of person to love living in an old home. We find that, more often than not, we have much in common with the homeowners. We all love art, music, being kind and, most telling of all, history.*

When we met the Thatchers, we knew we would be longtime friends. They are happy, loving and appreciative people. They love their house for what it is and do not mourn what it might be missing. An old house is never perfect—it has its rough edges, imperfect and uneven floors and cracking walls.

The foundations aren't made with cement and rebar yet they've stood the test of time. So much of this can be compared to people in general—we aren't perfect, but we have character and quirks, things that make us all unique.

 OLD HOMES OFTEN REMIND
US TO SLOW DOWN AND ENJOY
SIMPLE THINGS.

## KITCHEN PERSONALITY

The kitchen has original beadboard and an overhead beam. A
pendant light hanging over the table, while vintage looking, is new
and stylish right now.

**BOLD COLORS**
Bright colors can bring old homes to life.
Here pops of blue and orange mix well with a
subtler green.

# Angles That Add Interest

Sometimes it's hard to put a finger on why a space feels like it has character. *Is it the moldings, the floor, the lights?* Is it the paint color or the patina?

Attic space is one of those old-home features that is fun to re-imagine. They have so many different angles, nooks and crannies. The interest that the slanted walls create is difficult to achieve in other ways. This attic is particularly interesting because it is covered in beadboard and painted in such a wonderful warm tone.

When these homes were built, the attics were not generally finished. They were where the boys slept, and attic rooms weren't meant to be seen. Now we want to use every inch of space available, so making good use of the attic is a natural place to add valuable and beautiful square footage.

Although the floor-to-ceiling cabinet on the right is new, it fits *perfectly* with this hundred-year-old antique wood cabinet with marble top and back. It's not always more difficult to give something personality; *it just sometimes takes more thought.*

A FAMILY HOME

# THE HEALING HOUSE

*We name most of our houses—they are like children to us. When we bought this home from an amazing and loving family, they explained that it had been in their family since it was built and has been a place where their family has come after difficult times. They called it the Healing House, and we have called it that ever since.*

It is such a touching sentiment to know that a home can be a place to heal and feel love. We believe that historic homes have many stories to tell about the people who have lived in them. People ask us all the time if we have ever felt anything "negative" or "scary" in them: the answer is no. No matter how bad of shape a home is in, we add so much positivity and love to them that we only feel happiness while working there.

**ARCHITECTURAL SALVAGE**
We have a love-hate relationship with architectural salvage. On one hand, we love that we can use it to re-create character (like that around this door), but on the other hand, it makes us sad to think about the home that lost the piece.

 We love using inexpensive materials to make a big impact, like standard subway tile and cement-veneer DIY countertops.

**HOW TO**

To achieve this look we first painted the stairs with chalkboard paint and then covered them with a lightweight printed vinyl of an old masters painting we had printed at a local sign shop. We then cut it to size and applied it to each step, not worrying if it was too perfect.

 WE ARE NEVER AFRAID TO ADD SOMETHING FUN AND UNEXPECTED TO AN OLD HOME.

# Modern Meets Historic

The Healing House has been an enjoyable place to *mix modern looks with historic features*, as with the stairway on the previous overleaf.

In this house, there were existing 1960s cabinets that were in good shape. We kept them, even though they were a little more modern than what we would have made custom. We painted them a muted gray ("Revere Pewter" by Benjamin Moore) to support the gray concrete veneer countertop. This house feels fun and fresh, so we are happy with the addition of more modern elements.

**DIY COUNTERTOPS**
Cement countertops are something you can do yourself. Simply spread Ardex feather finish with a metal trowel, sanding between several coats.

ARTS AND CRAFTS

# KLEINER HOME

*Nestled in a beautiful suburban neighborhood, this perfectly preserved and maintained Arts and Crafts home stands as a symbol of history, great taste and aesthetics. Sadly, many of its neighbors are being torn down to make homes that are much larger and only made to look old.*

Despite the temptation of having more square footage and amenities with a new build, the Kleiners are extremely committed to their historic home and have spent a lot of time and care making it their own. They are very mindful of its time period but also love filling it with things that matter to them. They have an extensive Arts and Crafts pottery collection and are avid art collectors.

**IDYLLIC SETTING**
It can take years for a yard to look this perfect. Old houses often come with the bonus of a mature landscape.

## BEAUTIFUL NOOKS

Open-concept floor plans have become very popular lately, and while we
do appreciate having large groups of people over, we love the intimacy that
little nooks in old homes create.

## UNIQUE SPACES

This is not a normal room; you have to step up the stairs and go through an arch—it's much more than just an opening to the dining room. Antique period furnishings amplify the tone of this home. The fireplace and mantel detail are original.

## AUTHENTIC STYLING

An authentic period chandelier replaced a missing one.
The collection of pottery is breathtaking in its simplicity
and the colors are gorgeous.

## ORIGINAL BATHROOMS

It is rare to have original bathrooms in a restored historic home. These lovely turquoise tiles have a natural crackling and patina that is extremely hard to replicate. When we find a bathroom in this good of condition, we think twice before deciding that an update is necessary.

Above is a detail of one antique rug. Wonderful original details *make this master bedroom a beautiful retreat.* A Gothic arched door with leaded glass and crystal doorknobs are key features difficult and expensive to replicate today. Elements like this make a historic house *even more special.*

 MATURE LANDSCAPES ARE A VALUABLE

ASSET OF HISTORIC HOMES.

*Don't be tempted to chop down old or "junk" trees just to clear them out.*

*There is a great deal to be said for the privacy that a yard like this provides.*

INVITING AND PEACEFUL

# GIBBONS HOUSE

*This home is full of unique details; original brick and pristine painted shutters and trim are among our favorites. The welcoming front porch that spreads across the main part of the home anchors it and invites guests to sit a while and enjoy.*

Inside the home are some amazing original details, like the coved ceiling and wood banister. The inlaid floors are a pure work of art and the brightness of the home makes it feel both open and cozy at the same time.

**UNPAINTED BRICK**

Sometimes it's hard to know when it's okay to paint brick. Our general rule is: if it was built before 1950, we don't.

## BRIGHTENING YOUR SPACE

An Arts and Crafts home doesn't have to be over the top or filled with dark woods and furniture. The owners have taken a more modern approach with light walls. The floor is original; notice the inlay around the edges of the room.

*This stove nook is full of character.* We love the arch, subway tile and the lights on either side. Details like these really set old homes apart. *Built-in banquette seating*, original to this historic home, is popular again.

**EMBRACING ORIGINAL TILE**
We love original tile and the patina that it can develop. Almost all old
tile can be brought back to life with some good scrubbing and buffing.

ADOBE PIONEER HOME

# RUBY'S HOUSE

*Candis grew up near this home and always admired it. It belonged to Max and Ruby, two happy and lovely people. They raised their family here and loved the time they spent in this home. They had done an extensive remodel sometime before 1980 but admitted that they weren't enthusiasts of the Victorian look.*

One day Candis asked Ruby about the house. Candis had been working on Three-Twenty-Three (her first historic remodel) and was looking for inspiration in old houses; this home had been built around the same time. She asked about the trim inside and Ruby said, "The first thing I did was rip out those old mopboards!" Candis just had to laugh. It's important to remember that not everybody sees old houses in the same way.

It is fun to honor the memories made here while still working to make the home a little more true to its origin. We are excited to show Ruby the new old mopboards that we are going to re-create.

**125 YEARS OF MEMORIES**
We want to preserve as much of this home as we possibly can. We are keeping the original adobe exposed and rebuilding the front porch to look more like it did when it was first built.

**PROTECTING THE ADOBE BRICK**

The original adobe brick on this home has been exposed to the elements for the past 125 years, but very little wear has shown. We plan on keeping it exposed and protecting it with a good drip edge on the roof and efficient gutters.

Even though we haven't started our renovation on Ruby's House, *we still think it is beautiful as it is*. It has one of the most intact primitive early Utah adobe brick exteriors we've seen. It is a great example of mature trees enhancing a property—*things we absolutely love in an old home!* We plan on adding new "old" English trim that is a little more like what would have been there originally and a more *ornate front porch*.

## ALMOST LOST FOREVER
# THE SKYLINE HOUSE

*We are often asked to share what the "worst" home we've ever restored was—hands down, it was the Skyline house. It was absolutely in shambles when we bought it and this 1800s beauty was slated for demolition. (We call it Skyline because its roofline perfectly mimics the skyline of the mountains behind it.)*

You never know why a beautiful historic home becomes neglected. It's very hard for us to imagine ever taking out original trim or doors, ripping up floors or knocking down original walls. It's almost like a disease: once it starts, it's so hard to cure. It takes someone dedicated to historic preservation to love it back to life.

Skyline had sat vacant and ready for demolition for more than two years by the time we were the owners. The roof covering had been removed and it was exposed to the elements. The floors had been ripped out and all of the original features were gone. We restored the home over the course of three months and it has been one of our most fulfilling projects to date. We sold it to a wonderful family, the Squires. They are our good friends and "old homies," and we couldn't imagine Skyline having better caretakers.

**FAMILY TIME**

It had been a long time since this home had heard the happy pitter-patter of little feet. The Squires feel like this house was always meant to be theirs and we couldn't agree more.

When we restore a home, we don't make it perfect. We once spent hours upon hours caulking, puttying, priming and painting a soffit made of beadboard. It *literally looked brand new.* There was an intense moment of loss for us when we finished. Now we like to leave things looking *just old enough.*

Even though Skyline was built in the 1800s, we didn't necessarily want to make it a High Victorian cottage. We decided to take a somewhat Spanish approach to the design to pay homage to the town of Springville, Utah, where the home is located. Springville has a number of Spanish Revival homes and we liked giving a little bit of that look to Skyline.

 A BRIGHT KITCHEN CAN BRING NEW LIFE
TO ANY OLD HOME.

**W**E HAD NEVER SEEN A BATHROOM THIS BAD BEFORE. It had rotted and deteriorated to almost an unrecognizable state when we acquired the home. The only thing left intact was the original cast-iron tub and some usable floor trusses.

After a month of just getting the space to the point where you could walk on the floors, we were able to start piecing back original and re-created details. We added this Eastlake mirror that is rumored to have hung in the home of the outlaw Jesse James. Looking at this space now, it's hard to imagine that it was almost demolished and lost forever!

### SHOWING THE BONES OF AN OLD HOME

We often remove the plaster ceiling from a vault to expose the underlying 2 x 4 beams, then insulate and drywall up into the roof vault. We don't clean them up too much; they become a great focal point for a room—mixing old with new.

Embracing and accentuating the *natural and underlying* building materials is part of our renovation style. Victorians would probably think we were crazy for exposing beams in this way, but it is a testament to the *amazing structure that historic buildings have.* We love being able to see the rough edges in a home along with the polished.

It's exciting to see the families we sell these houses to make them their own. The Squire family *cherish their home; they fill it with love and happiness every day.*

That is a large part of why we do what we do. We want people to enjoy these homes again. *We want new memories to be made and remembered here.* Preserving this history is a great responsibility that we are all too happy to take on.

# Simple Is Sometimes Best

When we bought Skyline, we were thrilled to have an original fireplace mantel perfectly centered between two windows. It was covered in a 1970s tile surround and looked horrible, but we were excited for the challenge of making it look its best again.

The original plan was to putty, caulk and sand the mantel, then have a marble insert piece made to fit inside over the tile. Instead, we decided to take a chance and see what was underneath. It was late at night and we barely had any light, but when we started to pull off the tile, we were *ecstatic* to see the original brick still intact underneath!

Sometimes all an old house needs is to be taken back to its most simple structure and let its true beauty stand out.

### BORROWING CHARACTER

The banister in the hallway came from a section of Love House's railing that was removed when we created a laundry room. It's so fun to have a little piece of its history live on here. The natural patina of this wood is inside the mudroom at Skyline; we painted a matte polyurethane on it to keep it looking this way forever.

## A HOME MEANT FOR CREATIVITY

# THE BANISTER HOUSE

*We had been searching, like always, for a new project to take on when we came across the most amazing, nearly intact 1800s home. We put an offer in; it was accepted and then later rejected by the bank. They said they wanted a buyer that was planning on living there, not "an investor." We were heartbroken and worried about who would buy it—who would love it as much as we did.*

About a month later, we noticed an adorable family outside. We stopped and met a kind, humble and endearing family, the Liddiards! They had purchased the home and we could see that they had the same respect and excitement for this home as we did—maybe even more!

They named it the Banister House after the original family (the Banisters) and they have been slowly renovating it back to life. It has been such a joy to become friends with this incredible family and to see them enjoy and care for this home.

**MODERN HISTORIC**

Old homes can feel fresh and modern with the right decor. Mixing modern art and antique rugs is a great way to update a historic space.

**USING PAINT TO ADD CHARACTER**
White painted floors downstairs make it
feel fresh and modern. We absolutely love
the cabinet painted blue.

## KIDS LIVE HERE TOO

The dining room is kid friendly, with places for homework and play as well as preparing and eating meals. The chalkboard wall is the Liddiard family hub.

# Let your home be happy.

*Old homes are not meant to be museums. They are places for children and adults alike to let their imaginations grow.*

 This home may have looked *outdated and neglected* before, but with a little bit of cleaning and paint, it has a *whole new life—a very happy and fun life!*

**HANDMADE HOME**
Kids' rooms add a lot of life to historic homes, especially when filled with toys that are classic or handmade.

Merrilee Liddiard, is an extremely talented artist and illustrator. The master bedroom that she shares with her husband, Jon, is filled with her whimsical illustrations and projects.

Not every home has to have rooms upon rooms for different tasks. Here the *master bedroom* doubles as an *office and studio*.

### EVERY DING AND SCRATCH TELLS A STORY

This incredible banister has been left almost entirely original, full of imperfections and patina. The original doors, upper right, were faux painted 120 years ago to look like expensive grained wood. The Liddiards like to showcase the family's personality with playful objects and art, facing.

A TREASURED PAST

# ORSON HYDE HOME

*It was such an honor to be invited to showcase this home, which belonged to Orson Hyde, a prominent figure in Utah pioneer and settlement history. The home underwent an extensive renovation by the current homeowners, where they made every effort to love it back to life. Again, we have become fast friends with them and are impressed with their dedication to the home's restoration.*

It wasn't as simple as repairing plaster and painting walls. This home had not been given the time and attention it needed over the years. The homeowners saw the potential it had and spent endless hours meticulously restoring original features and repainting the historical finish.

The result is almost magical. The doors, trim and floors may look even better than the day they were originally finished, due to the exceptional talent of the artisan painter. We think Orson would be very pleased with the work that has been done.

**HYDE HOME IN THE 1800S**
It is always such a treat to have original photographs of a historical home. This picture on display is a reminder of the pride the original owners had for their home.

Bathrooms can be a challenge in older homes. We want all of the *modern conveniences* but also insist on historical integrity. New claw-foot tubs and beadboard are a perfect mix of the two periods, bringing both *comfort and style to a new old space.*

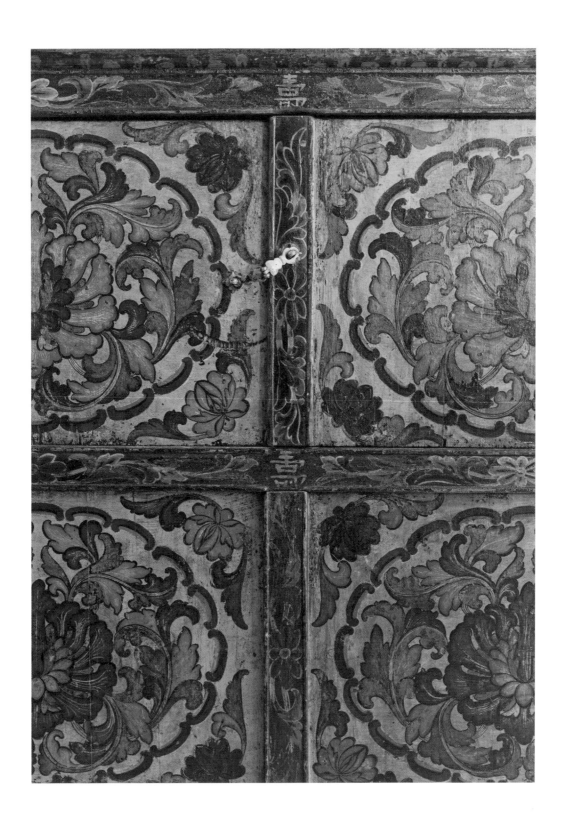

LET ANTIQUE FURNITURE
ADD DIMENSION AND COLOR TO
YOUR HOME.

**EXPOSED STONE**
This back kitchen addition, facing, has been added by the new owners. The original outdoor wall is now indoors. Shelves have been built where a window used to be.

 The homeowners absolutely love antique and historic things, *especially quilts.* Their extensive collection throughout the home adds colorful impact to the rooms. Decorating with *whimsical and timeless pieces* makes for a layered and classic look.

## THE RIGHT KIND OF FAUX PAINTING

The door has been faux painted to look like mahogany. The tall cabinet, facing, was
found in pieces and was rebuilt and restored. It took more than a year to put it back
together from its nearly splintered state.

A small bathroom has been creatively
tucked into an unused space.

**TONE-ON-TONE**

One of our favorite things about old homes was their use of subtle color. They didn't have mountains of paint color choices as we do today; in fact, a hundred years ago there were fewer than a dozen or so. We love the use of tone-on-tone color to accentuate the lovely woodwork and plaster walls, as seen here.

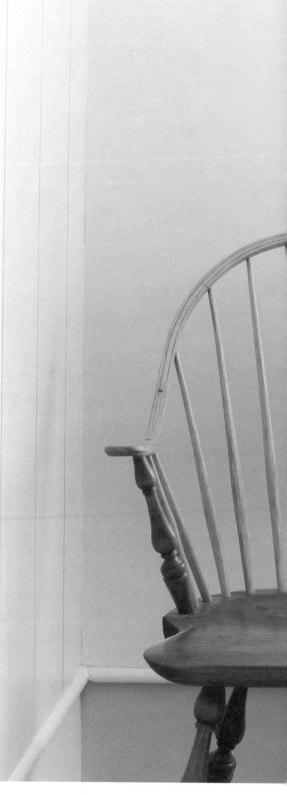

### EXQUISITE NEW CRAFTSMANSHIP

The bathroom upstairs is new, but the homeowners have added details that make it seem like it has always been there. This window bench, center, is a modern piece that has been expertly crafted to resemble an antique. It is a true treasure in the home. The door hardware really stands out in simple contrast.

A FAMILY TREASURE

# SMOOT FAMILY HOME

*It is absolutely rare for a historical home today to still belong to the original family. The Smoot house is an incredible example of a legacy of dedication and love for their home, which they have meticulously maintained throughout many decades.*

When we met the Smoot family, we were in awe of their appreciation for their home. They have lived here all of their lives and plan to pass the home to their children as well. The walls showcase portraits of their ancestors, the original owners, and they have been careful to honor their memory while still making the home their own.

They don't feel stifled living here; they have made some changes but have left most everything intact, modernizing only what was necessary. The feeling we had upon walking into this home was an immense sense of a time passed but not lost. People like the Smoots make our hearts swell as we realize there are other families who care as much as we do about old homes.

**THE GRAND FRONT PORCH**
The original front porch has been thoughtfully preserved and repaired when needed. The Smoots had historical tile reproduced when some were damaged and they have kept almost everything else original.

SMOOT FAMILY HOME

**ANCESTORS LIVING ON**

Paintings of their own ancestors, who also lived in the home, is a luxury that many owners of historic homes don't have. The family adds to the antiques by bringing in different pieces, but they rarely take away.

**HEN A FAMILY IS LUCKY ENOUGH** to pass a home down through the generations, an amazing spirit of family pride can grow within the home. The Smoot home is furnished with ancestral heirlooms mixed with antiques. This chair, above, is a family piece that still wears the original mohair upholstery. It is remarkable to see the great-great-great-grandchildren still enjoying their ancestral home to this day.

## INLAID FLOORS
These original inlaid floors are some of the most beautiful we have ever seen—
a testament to exceptional craftsmanship. The thin outline detail is almost too
much to comprehend.

The family library at the Smoot house is filled with volumes from the past
and present. *There is a palpable sense of history here.* The adjustable-arm
lamp is great for reading and the Craftsman sofa with leather cushions is
classic. *Imagine what it must be like* to live in a such a place, knowing that
your ancestors walked the same floors.

## TRUE TO THE ORIGINAL

The kitchen, facing, is fairly small but charming—a perfect place to eat breakfast. Dinner is served in the grand dining room. The staircase has hand-carved details and original finish. Think how many people have touched this newel post over the course of a century.

TO BE ABLE TO ADD YOUR
HISTORY, EXPERIENCES
AND STORY TO AN
OLD HOME IS AN HONOR.

SMOOT FAMILY HOME

*Passed down through generations.*

### STEPPING BACK IN TIME

The original wood door surrounds and leather-like wallpaper look very much the way they did a century ago. The staircase in this home is one of its grandest features.

OUR NEW OLD HOME

# LEMMON-DIXON HOUSE

*We were looking for an amazing historic home to do for our television show on HGTV when we came across the Lemmon-Dixon house. It was perfect—despite being in really bad shape, it had amazing original features begging to shine again. We didn't intend to live here when it was done, but we just couldn't help ourselves.*

This house was called the "big house" by the original owners. The husband was a sheep farmer and the wife was a shop owner and a very independent and self-sufficient woman. She loved this house and passed it on to her niece, Jennie. Jennie lived here the rest of her life and then it was sold to the only other owner besides us.

We treasure this home. We can't believe that we get to live with original pocket doors, ornate hardware and delicate moldings. We feel very proud that we were able to be the family that preserved and prepared this home for its next hundred years.

**ALMOST PRICELESS DOORS**
Just for fun we had a door craftsman come and look at the doors to see what they would cost to replicate. He estimated that it would be about $3,500 for the singles and $8,000 for the pocket doors. How lucky we are to have them.

Most people have some kind of association with old homes, be it their grandma's house that they loved (or hated) for different reasons or some other. Every home, new or old, should reflect your personality. We like to think that we are very modern Victorians living in the modern age.

Everything old can seem new again. This wallpaper from Sandberg is an antique pattern yet looks extremely modern.

## Tall Cabinets + Lighting

We basically get carte blanche when it comes to restoring kitchens. Historic kitchens usually consisted of a Hoosier cabinet, a wood burning stove and not much else. We have decided that a classic look for our homes is cabinets all the way to the ceiling—even if that means that they are seven feet tall. When people ask us if one needs a ladder to reach the top, we say, "You sure do!" Then we use simple lights to finish out a look that is enough on trend while still fitting in with original moldings and doors.

## Practicality + Beauty

Truly historic kitchens are not necessarily all that practical for how we live today. We can't cook on wood burning stoves (well, we *could*, but we don't want to) and we like putting our dishes in a machine to wash. We embrace what that means for our kitchens and we don't try to hide the fact that we have modern appliances and fixtures. When we can afford it, we make panels to cover them, but when we can't, we don't stress too much over it.

FAMILY HEIRLOOMS

We have so many things that are precious to us. This piano belonged to Candis's great-grandma and has been passed down to the oldest daughter for four generations. Our kids pull off the keys and play it too hard, but nothing can't be fixed. We believe in enjoying and using antiques (within reason, of course).

*We let our kids get messy in our house.* More often than not there are noodles or mac and cheese on our antique rugs, *and that's okay.*

## DIY CHARACTER

This was a plain wall before we decided to make our bedroom something special. Candis hand drew the pattern on graph paper, then we cut everything to scale and installed the molding to make picture frame molding and a chair rail. Now it looks like painted wood paneling and adds dimension to the room.

INDING UNUSED SPACE in an old home is such an exhilarating thing! When this house was built, the upstairs attic was meant to be used as storage—with beautiful molding around the window, of course. So when it was finished into usable space in 1920, they simply walled straight down and left these little nooks to act as insulation.

When we started renovating, we couldn't understand this "hallway to the window," so we opened it up to discover the most perfect place for two little beds, thanks to an addition of modern insulation. Although when we bought this house to restore, we never thought we would move into it, we couldn't help but picture little Kit with her best friend having sleepovers here. (As an aside, we always restore houses with the mind-set of what we would want if we lived there—which comes in handy, especially with this house.)

Our kids are used to hearing the words "from the 1800s," so they weren't surprised when we covered their ceiling in an 1830s star map.

### WALLPAPER IS NOT JUST FOR WALLS

We have a lot of kids (seven, to be exact) and we knew we needed a bunk room for at least four of them. It is perfectly nestled in a steeply pitched attic space that had been left unfinished since 1890. We had Rebel Walls print this amazing mural for the ceiling to get the biggest impact possible while keeping it simultaneously youthful and full of history. We've stayed up late making up stories about different constellations and letting our imaginations run wild.

### HISTORIC MOLDING

Although this part of the attic was never finished, we were very lucky to have the original trim around the windows. Most renovators tear it off, drywall behind and put it back on—but not us. We leave it in place and drywall *around* it. It just never seems to go back on in quite the same way. It's a little more work this way but worth the effort.

### REIMAGINED CHARACTER

We love the play between modern and historic with this Hygge & West wallpaper and original trim in the bathroom. We turned the former back porch, center, into a master bath complete with exposed brick and beadboard ceilings. Our vestibule, far right, features new Sandberg wallpaper and a beautiful new stained glass piece that we had crafted by Russ Peacock of Lehi, Utah.

Thank you for taking this journey with us. We love what we do and *have a true passion for restoring and preserving historic homes and buildings* for the next generation, for our children to love and appreciate. We hope that everyone can *enjoy the beauty* and heritage that old homes possess, and that together we can *make a difference in historic preservation.*

THE MAKING OF A BOOK

# Acknowledgments

*We absolutely could not have completed this work without our "village" of people. We feel so grateful to be surrounded by those who believe in our vision and share the same love for these historical homes and what they mean to all of us.*

## KEY CONTRIBUTORS

### Meta Coleman
@metacoleman_

Stylist, production designer and interior designer. Amazing taste, talent, work ethic and so much more.

### Chaunte Vaugn
@chauntevaughn

Our uber talented photographer and artist, able to capture every moment we had hoped for.

### Kirk and Eva Jorgenson
@sycamore_co

The most kind, calm and gracious producers who are also extremely talented artists in their own right.

### Zina Bennion
@momsstuffsalve

Our helpful and happy assistant who loves old houses, old people and old friends.

WE WOULD LIKE TO SINCERELY THANK our friends and family who have supported us on our borderline insane journey. We love you all so much and a sentence at the back of our book certainly can't express it enough. To Suzanne, Madge and the entire team at Gibbs Smith, who never doubted that we could make something amazing. To Meta Coleman and Chaunte Vaughn, who worked tirelessly to make everything look so amazing with their very particular commitment to beauty and art. Thank you to Kirk and Eva Jorgenson for keeping all of us alive and happy and to the many assistants and helpers who were there for us when we were overwhelmed, particularly Zina Bennion, Caitlin Watson Boyes, Jennifer Paul, Cammy Fuller, Kandyce Carroll and Emma Ellis. Thank you, thank you, thank you!

A special thanks to Bohem, The Green Ant, Tomorrow's House, Urban Vintage, Kerstin Grimmer, Michael and Jacqueline Coleman, Nicholas Coleman, Anthony's Fine Art and Antiques, Treasures Antique Mall, Sandberg Wallpaper, Rebel Walls, Hygge and West, Dwell Studio, Design Within Reach in Pasadena, Sun River Gardens, Sarah Winward, Mary Lee, ARQ, Kelly White, Helle Grimmer and Brittany Watson Jepsen.

Also, a sincere thank-you to those who opened their homes to us: Ronnie and Mikael Squire, Lee and Maurine Meredith, Sally Snow, Chris and Allison Anderson, Garbett Homes, the Goss Family, Joe Jackson, the Kleiners, the Morgan family, Otto Mileti, the Thatchers, the Barker family, the Smoot family and the Liddiards. We love you all!

And finally, thank you to our old homies, our fans. Without your support none of this would be possible. #saveanoldhouse

# RESOURCES

**Anthony's Fine Art and Antiques**
anthonysfineart.com
Unique European fine art and
antique furniture.

**Anthropologie**
anthropologie.com
Beautiful lamps and accessories, linens
and decorative objects.

**ARQ**
shoparq.com
Beautifully handcrafted, organic and
sustainable children's clothes and
accessories.

**Bohem**
bohem.co
Beautiful handcrafted rugs, textiles, bedding
and kitchen and bath accessories.

**Cactus and Tropicals**
cactusandtropicals.com
A selection of plants and flowers with
an impressive amount of large plants.

**Crate and Barrel**
crateandbarrel.com
Furniture, kitchen accessories.

**Dash and Albert**
dashandalbert.com
A large assortment of quality rugs and
classic designs.

**Design Within Reach**
dwr.com
Quality designer furniture, textiles, lighting
and accessories.

**Direct from Mexico**
directfrommexico.com
Beautiful handmade Mexican star lights and
accessories.

**Dwell Studio**
dwellstudio.com
Sophisticated bedding, furniture,
and lighting.

**Ferm Living**
fermliving.com
Danish-designed modern furnishings
and accessories.

**FLOR**
flor.com
Floor carpet tiles that we use in
kids' rooms.

**Green Ant**
thegreenant.com
Vintage, antique, midcentury, designer
furniture, lighting and accessories.

**House of Antique Hardware**
houseofantiquehardware.com
Beautiful reproduction hardware, drawer
pulls, handles, knobs, switch covers.

**Hygge and West**
hyggeandwest.com
Beautiful contemporary and
colorful wallpapers.

**Ikea**
ikea.com
Kitchen cabinets, countertops, dressers,
general furniture and decor.

**Muji**
muji.us or muji.com
Simple, well designed Japanese
home accessories.

**Pottery Barn**
potterybarn.com
Lights, rugs.

**Rebel Walls**
rebelwalls.com
A revolutionary wallpaper company that
allows you to print a mural from your own
image or use one from their collection.

**Sandberg Wallpaper**
sandbergwallpaper.com
A large collection of inspiring
Swedish wallpaper.

**Sarah Winward**
sarahwinward.com
Locally sourced, natural and beautifully
dynamic and creative floral arrangements.

**Sun River Gardens**
sunrivergardens.com
A wide assortment of house plants, trees,
flowers, pots and accessories.

**Target**
target.com
Our go-to for easy decorating pillows
and smalls.

**Tomorrow's House**
tomorrowshouse.info
Curated vintage, midcentury furniture,
lighting and accessories.

**Urban Vintage**
Salt Lake City, Utah
Reclaimed original antique furniture
and lighting.

**Treasures Antique Mall**
treasuresantiquemall.com
A large selection of antiques and vintage
pieces in Springville, Utah.

**West Elm**
westelm.com
Clean, contemporary textiles, furniture
and lighting.

Be nice to people. Do what you love.

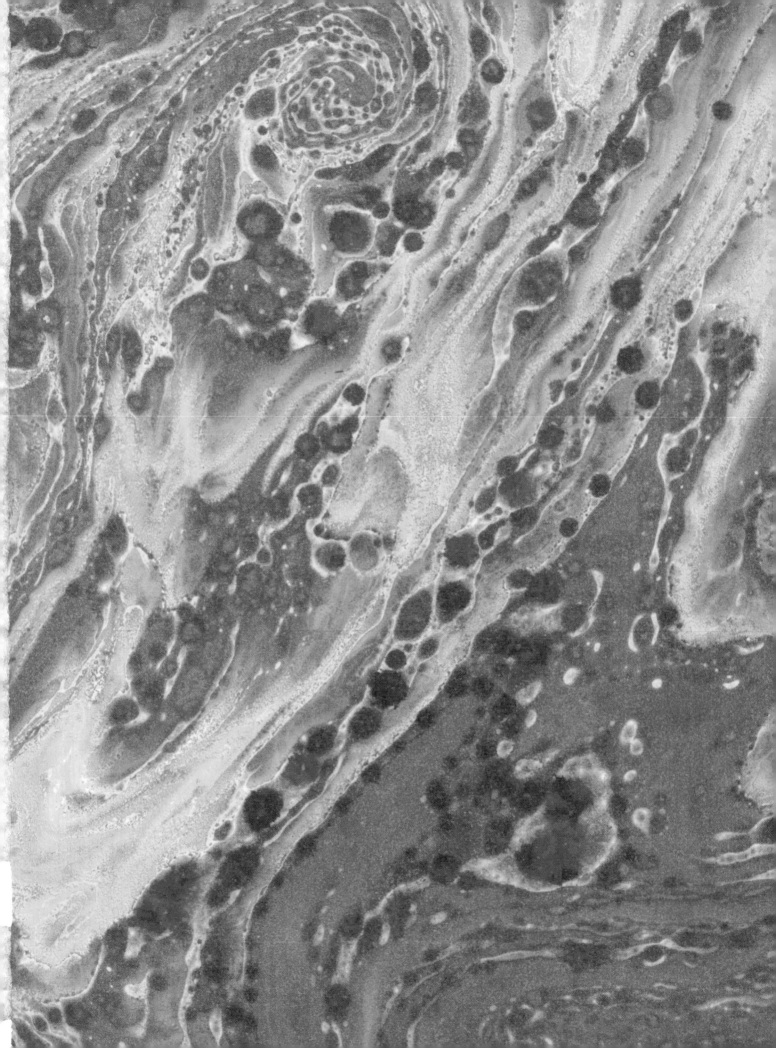

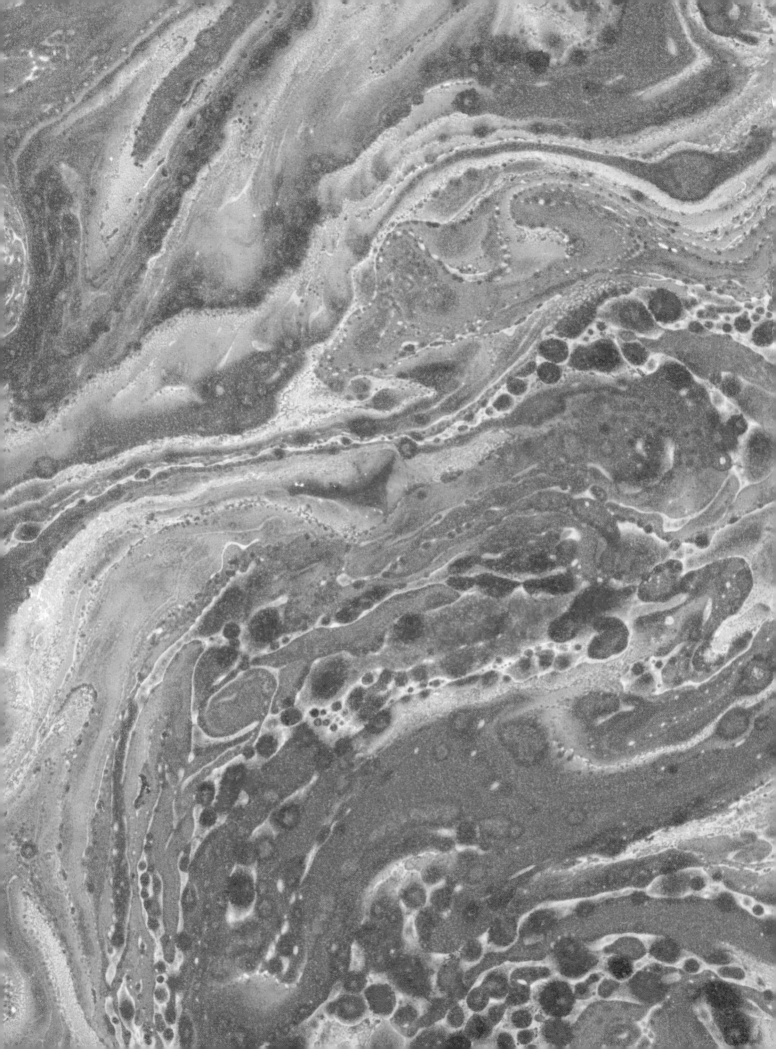